BRUTALLY GROSS JOKES

MORE GUT-BUSTING HUMOR FROM THE KING OF GROSS JOKES!

What do Polacks call Cheerios?

Donut seeds.

How do you spot a redneck at Sea World?

He's the one carrying a fishing pole.

What's the difference between garbage and an ugly girl?

Garbage gets picked up at least once a week.

Why don't cannibals eat Jewish kids?

Because they're always spoiled.

How do you pierce Oprah Winfrey's ears?

With a harpoon.

What's a transvestite's idea of a good time

To eat, drink, and be Mary.

BRUTALLY GROSS JOKES XXVI

Julius Alvin

Zebra Books
Kensington Publishing Corp.
http://www.zebrabooks.com

ZEBRA BOOKS are published by

Kensington Publishing Corp.
850 Third Avenue
New York, NY 10022

First Printing: April, 1998
10 9 8 7 6 5 4 3 2 1

Printed in the United States of America

CONTENTS

GROSS CELEBRITY JOKES

What do you call Roseanne holding a million dollars?

A cash cow.

What does O. J. Simpson have in common with Michael Jackson?

They both missed a glove and both were under the knife.

What's the name of Roseanne's new sitcom?

three-thirty-something.

What did Susan Smith's employer do when he found out she drowned her two children?

He docked her pay.

Did you hear that Marlee Martin and Helen Keller are doing comedy together?

It's called "Def Comedy Jam."

What happened when Ted Kennedy couldn't find his glasses?

He drank straight from the bottle.

What did Madonna do when she turned frigid?

She fucked her psychiatrist.

Why was Ted Bundy a bad golfer?

He always took a few slices before he put it in the hole.

How do you know when it's bedtime at Michael Jackson's house?

The big hand touches the little hand.

What do Branch Davidians and Wendy's hamburgers have in common?

They're both well done by Dave.

What's the difference between O. J. and Colonel Sanders?

Colonel Sanders kills his chicks before he batters them.

Hear about the new O. J. Simpson perfume?

You just slap it on.

What's the Spanish word for Rodney King?

Piñata.

Hear about the new Rodney King poker game?

Four clubs beat one spade.

Why does Bill Clinton have a clear conscience?

He's never used it.

What can Mark Fuhrman do that a black woman can't?

Get O. J. off.

How does Snow White get seven inches of cock?

One inch at a time.

What do you get when you cross a convertible and Madonna?

A singer whose top comes right off.

Why are Michael Jackson's pants so short?

Because they're not his.

Why did Michael Jackson give up Pepsi?

He switched to Seven & Up.

What's green, lies in a ditch, and smells like shit?

A dead Girl Scout.

A GROSS GRAB BAG

A five-year-old child crawls onto Santa's lap at the local Wal-Mart.

Santa asks the five-year-old, "And what do you want for Christmas, little girl?"

The kid replies, "I want a Barbie and a G.I. Joe."

"But little girl, Barbie doesn't come with G.I. Joe," Santa says.

"Yes, she does," the little girl insists.

"Barbie doesn't come with G.I. Joe, she comes with Ken," Santa tells her.

"No," the little girl says. "Barbie does come with G.I. Joe. She only fakes it with Ken."

So three mice are sitting in a bar.

The first mouse says, "I'm so tough, I stole the cheese from the mousetrap before the trap slammed down on my neck." He knocks back a shot of bourbon.

The second mouse says, "You know those little mouse tablets that kill us on sight? I'm so tough, I ate one of 'em whole!" He, too, knocks back a shot of bourbon.

The third mouse slips off his barstool and starts to walk out of the bar. The first mouse asks him, "Hey, where are you going?"

The third mouse replies, "I'm going home to fuck the cat."

Why are students frisked in the New York City public schools?

So they can give you a gun if you don't already have one.

How can you tell when a chick has been jerking off with a cucumber?

When the salad comes, so does she.

How do you know when you're really a loser?

On your wedding night, your bride says she wants to date other men.

How does a guy know when he's really in love?

He divorces his wife.

Why do women like men who've pierced their ears?

They've experienced pain and bought jewelry.

So the third grader comes running home from school. He bursts into the family double-wide and says to his mother, "Mama, we all went swimming today."

Mama says, "That's nice, Billy Bob."

"And you know what, Mama? I got me the biggest pecker in the whole third-grade class."

"I ain't surprised, son," his mother remarks.

"Why's that, Mama?"

"I reckon," his mother says, "it's cause you're seventeen."

What do you call a bleached blonde standing on her head?

A brunette with bad breath.

So then there's this guy whose penis is too long—his girlfriend can't handle it. As it turns out, he also has a terrible stuttering problem.

He goes to see his doctor, who says, "Your stutter is caused by the fact that your dick is too long. If I cut four inches off it, both of your problems will be solved."

The guy tells his doctor, "Let's give it a try."

A week later, the guy comes back and says, "Doc, it only half worked. My stutter is gone, but my girlfriend says my dick isn't big enough to satisfy her. Maybe you'd better give me back those four inches."

The doctors says, "F-F-Fuck you."

How do you know when you're at a high-class wedding in Tennessee?

The bride's veil covers most of her overalls.

How many rednecks does it take to screw in a lightbulb?

What's a lightbulb?

What's the difference between a lawyer and a prostitute?

A prostitute stops fucking you when you're dead.

Do you know how to save a lawyer from drowning?

If you don't, good!

What's the difference between a Harley and a Hoover vacuum cleaner?

The position of the dirt bag.

What do you get when you cross a lesbian and a lawyer?

An attorney who won't fuck you.

So a rabbi, a priest, and a lawyer are on a sinking ship. As they try to find a lifeboat, the rabbi says, "Children first!"

The lawyer says, "Fuck the children!"

The priest says, "Do you think we have time?"

So a housewife, an accountant, and a lawyer are asked how much two plus two equals.

The housewife says, "Four."

The accountant says, "I'm not sure. Let me run those figures through my spreadsheet one more time."

The lawyer lowers his voice and says, "How much do you want it to be?"

Why do women fake orgasms?

Because they think we care.

What do you call a lawyer with an IQ of 50?

Your Honor.

So your mother-in-law and your lawyer are trapped in a burning building, and you only have time to save one of them. What do you do?

Go catch a movie.

How do you know a Deadhead's been to your house?

He's still there.

Hear about the flasher who was thinking about retiring?

He decided to stick it out a little longer.

So God is trying to decide where to go on vacation. He remarks to one of his angels, "I just don't know where to go. I've been everywhere."

The angel says, "I hear Alpha Centauri's nice this time of year."

God says, "I've been there."

"How about Mars?" the angel asks.

"I went there last year," God replies.

"How about Earth?" the angel inquires.

"Nah," God says. "The last time I was there I knocked up this Jewish chick and they're still talking about it."

What has four balls and eats ants?

Two uncles.

How do you get a nun pregnant?

Dress her up like an altar boy.

What's the difference between meat and fish?

When you beat your fish, it dies.

What comes after 69?

Listerine.

GROSS ETHNIC JOKES

Hear about the Jewish American Princess with leprosy?

She talked her head off.

What about the Puerto Rican who was too young to drive?

He stole taxis.

What's the difference between an Irishman and a Muslim?

An Irishman gets stoned before he sleeps with someone else's wife.

What did the guy do after his Italian wife left him?

He masturbated with a Brillo pad.

How did the Jewish American Princess commit suicide?

She jumped off her credit cards.

How ugly was the Italian girl?

Even a leech wouldn't give her a hickey.

What's the definition of a virgin in Harlem?

A girl whose mother is too ugly to have a boyfriend.

How do Polish women remove their make-up?

With Easy-Off.

What is JAP aerobics?

Shopping faster.

How can you spot a JAP at an orgy?

She's the one who says, "What, my turn again?"

How can you spot the Italian parents at a PTA meeting?

They're the ones attending under an assumed name.

How can you tell when a woman is half Irish and half Italian?

She mashes potatoes with her feet.

What does a Polish girl put behind her ears to attract men?

Her knees.

Why do Mexicans eat refried beans?

So they can get a second wind.

Why did the Irishman like to drink and drive?

He ran into the most interesting people.

How can you spot the WASP kid in the playground?

He's the one making mudpies with a Cuisinart.

So the Polish woman was allergic to birth control pills. She asked her gynecologist to recommend the best contraceptives.

The doctor said, "Try withdrawal, douches, and rubbers."

Three years later, the Polish woman was walking down the street with three children when she ran into her gynecologist, who said to her, "I see you didn't take my advice."

"I tried," the Polish woman said. "Stan here was a pullout, Stosh was a washout, and Vladimir was a blowout."

Hear about the black kid who got promoted to the second grade?

He was so excited, he cut himself shaving.

What's made out of metal and glass and comes in 5,000 pieces?

A car in Belfast.

Why did the Polack marry his dog?

Because he had to.

How do you keep a Polack from biting his nails?

Make him wear shoes.

Why are Catholic girls so quiet during sex?

They don't believe in talking to strangers.

Hear about the Polish duck hunters?

The decoy got away.

So a Jewish guy took his wife on a camping trip. As they sat around the campfire one night, a huge animal burst into the clearing. The Jew and his wife started running away. The wife cried out, "What the hell is it, a bear?"

The Jew, five yards ahead of his wife, yelled back, "How should I know? I'm in textiles, not furs!"

What do you get when you cross an Irishman with a German?

Someone who's too drunk to follow orders.

Hear about the Polish athlete?

He'd give his right arm to be ambidextrous.

Hear about the Klansman from Alabama?

He was a real sheethead.

Why did the Irish cancel St. Patrick's Day?

They dug him up and discovered he died from AIDS.

Why don't cannibals eat Jewish kids?

They're always spoiled.

Why are turtleneck sweaters so popular in Poland?

They hide the flea collars.

Hear about the Polack who won the lottery?

He bought a Winnebago with a wine cellar.

Hear about the new dance club in Israel?

It's called "Let My People Go-Go."

Where do black folks buy toys for their children?

FAO Schwartze.

So this black guy walks into a saloon accompanied by a big gorilla. The black guy says to the bartender, "Gimme two beers."

The bartender takes one look at the gorilla and says to the black guy, "Get the hell out of here. I don't serve gorillas in this place."

The black guy goes home, taking the gorilla with him. Once there, he shaves all the fur off the gorilla, then dresses the animal in a tight red dress and high heels.

The black guy goes back to the bar with the gorilla. He says to the bartender, "Gimme two beers."

The bartender gives the black guy two beers. The black guy takes the beers and, with the gorilla, goes to a table in the back.

The bartender says to a friend, "Ain't it always the case? A beautiful Italian girl walks in, and she's with a nigger."

Why did the Polish scientist stay up night after night?

He was trying to find a cure for insomnia.

Why is teen sex in Bosnia so exciting?

You never know if the car is going to explode before you do.

What do you call a fag from Tokyo?

A Japansie.

What do you call the alphabet in Harlem?

The impossible dream.

How can you tell when a bride is Jewish?

They pick up the rice after the wedding.

Why don't Serbs go out to bars anymore?

They get bombed at home.

Why do pigeons fly upside down over Harlem?

There's nothing worth shitting on.

A REALLY GROSS VARIETY

How do you know when a hospital patient has AIDS?

He gets his shots with a dart gun.

What's the difference between a wife and Jell-O?

Jell-O moves when you eat it.

How long do rednecks cook their meat?

Until the skid marks don't show.

Why do women have legs?

So you don't have to drag them into the bathroom to wash up after sex.

What's the true definition of child abuse?

A mother who dips her baby's thermometer in BENGAY.

What's the difference between a congressman and happiness?

Money can't buy happiness.

What do women and condoms have in common?

They both spend more time in your wallet than on your dick.

So the elderly couple died in a car accident and went straight to heaven. They were given a tour by St. Peter himself. St. Peter said, "Over here is your oceanside condominium. Right there are the tennis courts, and next to them is the golf course. The swimming pool is over there. If you need any refreshments, just push the first button you see."

When St. Peter left, the old man turned to his wife, "Shit, Helen, this is your fault."

"What do you mean?" the wife asked.

"If it wasn't for you and your lousy oat bran," the husband complained, "we could have been here five years ago!"

A ten-year-old kid asks his mother, "Is God black or white?"

His mother responds, "Son, God is both black and white."

The kid then asks, "Mom, is God a man or a woman?"

His mother replies, "God is both a man and a woman."

The kid now asks, "Mom, is God straight or gay?"

"God is both straight and gay," the mother says.

"Mom," the kid finally asks, "is God Michael Jackson?"

Why do bachelors like smart women?

Because opposites attract.

What's the best thing about masturbating?

You always have a good grip on yourself.

How can you spot the Jewish baby in a nursery?

He's the one with heartburn.

What do you give the man who has everything?

A woman to show him how to do it.

Why are parrots smarter than chickens?

There's no such thing as Kentucky Fried Parrot.

What's the last thing a tramp from New Jersey takes off?

Her bowling shoes.

How many men does it take to change a roll of toilet paper?

Who gives a shit?

Why did the gay pickpocket always come home empty-handed?

He was just browsing.

GROSS
GAY AND LESBIAN JOKES

What do you call two lesbians in a canoe?

Fur traders.

Hear about the JAP who was bisexual?

Twice a year was too much.

Hear about the gay termite?

He went for the woodpecker.

Why did the gay golfer go to Puerto Rico?

He wanted a hole in Juan.

Hear about the gay Canadian mountie?

He not only gets his man, he gets to keep him.

So this gay couple get into a fight and break up. As Bruce is packing, he says to Stanley, "And I'm taking all the Streisand CDs with me."

"Well, you know what you can do with them!" Stanley says.

"Don't you dare try making up with me."

Why do gay men grow mustaches?

To hide their stretch marks.

Why did the fag get fired from his job at the sperm bank?

He was caught drinking on the job.

Hear about the queer Dutch boy who stuck his finger in a dyke?

She beat the crap out of him.

What's the difference between lesbians and whales?

No one is trying to save the lesbians.

What's a fag's favorite dish at a Chinese restaurant?

Sum yung guy.

Why did the Jewish lesbian move to Israel?

She missed the Hebrew tongue.

Hear about the transvestites who got arrested?

They were booked for male fraud.

Then there was the guy who gave his first blow job.

He woke up with a queer taste in his mouth.

What's the definition of hell on earth?

A blind lesbian in a fish store.

So the Jewish fag says to his roommate, "Sidney, did the rabbi come yet?"

"No," the roomie says, "but he's starting to moan."

Hear about the gay Polack?

He liked women.

Why did the gay security guard get fired?

He was bending over on the job.

What did the lesbian bumper sticker say?

"Save a tree. Eat a beaver."

What's a lesbian's favorite pet?

A lap dog.

Hear about the popsicle for queers?

It's got hair around the stick.

NOW THAT'S SICK!

A man rushes into a saloon and starts knocking back shots of Jack Daniels, as fast as the bartender can pour them.

"Trying to drown your sorrows?" the bartender asks.

"Yes, I am," the man admits.

"Take my advice, buddy, it doesn't work," the bartender tells him.

"You're telling me?" the man replies. "I can't get that damn kid to go anywhere near the water!"

So Ed goes to see a psychiatrist to complain about his oversexed girlfriend.

Ed says, "My Sheila will stop at nothing to satisfy her lustful, kinky desires and bottomless sexual cravings. What can I do?"

The shrink says, "Tell her to make an appointment with me immediately."

Hear about the Australian guys who came late to the gay Olympics?

They couldn't get out of Sidney.

What goes in stiff but comes out soft?

Wrigley's Spearmint.

Why did the JAP write her zip code on her belly?

So her lover would come faster.

What's the definition of a Tampax?

Clitty-litter.

Then there was the ninety-year-old man who married a twenty-year-old girl.

All his friends had it in for him.

So little Timmy the Boy Scout comes home with a hand grenade in his pants. His mother says to him, "What's that in your trousers?"

Timmy answers, "A hand grenade."

His mother inquires, "Why do you have a hand grenade in your pants?"

"The next time the scoutmaster tries to grab my cock, I'll blow his fucking fingers off," Timmy declares.

So the Polish housewife tried to surprise her husband on his birthday by putting on a pair of crotchless panties. When her mate came home, she was lying on the rug, spreading her legs. "You want some of this?" she asked.

"Shit no," the Polack said. "Look what it's done to your undies."

What was the lesbian's favorite ice cream flavor?

Sardine.

How do you know when your wife is really ugly?

The waiter puts her plate on the floor.

How do you know when your kid's really a sadist?

He gets a girl pregnant just so he can watch the rabbit die.

Why are men like lawn mowers?

They're hard to get started, and they only work half the time.

What's the definition of a true genius?

A nudist with a memory for faces.

So Murray goes to see his physician, who gives him an X ray, blood tests, and an EKG, followed by another half-dozen tests.

"Murray," the doctor begins, "I've got good news and I've got bad news."

"What's the good news?" Murray wants to know.

"The good news is, my son just got accepted to Harvard law school."

"And what's the bad news?" Murray asks.

"You're going to pay for it."

Why did the Polack throw away his toilet brush?

It hurt his asshole too much.

How do you know when your parents hate you?

The house catches on fire, and they send you inside to play.

What did the Jewish doctor tell the Arab who'd just taken an overdose of sleeping pills?

"Have a couple of drinks and get some rest."

Why do Polacks have arms?

So their fingers don't smell like armpits.

How do you know when you have a bad acne problem?

Your dog calls you Spot.

How do you know when there's something wrong with your local day care center?

Your kid plays strip poker at bath time.

What's the definition of a consultant?

A guy who knows fifty ways to screw but doesn't know any women.

So the bride and groom check into a motel on their wedding night. They're both young and very inexperienced.

They have sex, like it so much they get it on again, and end up screwing six more times before dawn.

As they're drifting off to sleep, the bride screams and starts crying.

"What's the matter, honey?" the groom asks.

She points to his shriveled up dick and cries, "Here we are, married one night, and we've already used it all up!"

What makes a bull sweat?

A tight jersey.

What's worse than a stranger sneezing in your face?

When he wipes his nose on your sleeve.

How does a necrophiliac beat the heat?

He goes to the morgue and has a cold one.

How do you play baseball in Mexico?

Drink some water and try to make it home.

The mother takes her five-year-old kid to the sporting goods store and says to the man working there, "I want to buy a baseball mitt for my son. How much do they cost?"

The clerk says, "Sixty dollars."

"That's way too much," the mother says. "How much is that bat?"

"Five dollars," the clerk says.

"I'll take it," the mother says.

As he's wrapping it up, the clerk says to her, "How about a ball for the bat?"

"No thanks," the mother says. "But I'll go down on you for the mitt."

Why is a blow job like chewing gum?

It's tough getting rid of the wad when you're done.

How do you know when your secretary is truly honest?

She calls in lazy.

What's the definition of a singles bar?

A place where girls go to look for husbands . . . and husbands go to look for girls.

What's the difference between love and insanity?

Insanity lasts forever.

How do you know when you're in a dyke bar?

Even the pool table doesn't have any balls.

Why did the blonde stay in the car wash for three hours?

She thought it was raining too hard to drive.

Why did Israel win the Six Day War so fast?

The tanks were rented.

Why do Italian women spend so much time in beauty parlors?

The estimates take three hours.

Why did the Jew marry the girl born on February 29?

So he'd only have to buy her a present every four years.

Why did the Polish photographer start collecting burnt-out lightbulbs?

He was building a darkroom.

How can you spot the redneck at Sea World?

He's the one carrying a fishing pole.

What happened when the nun got tired of using candles?

She called in an electrician.

An agent from the Internal Revenue Service goes to see an old lady to audit her tax returns for the last few years. As he's working, he notices a big bowl of almonds on her kitchen table.

He says to the old lady, "Mind if I have an almond?"

The old lady tells him, "Of course not, help yourself."

The auditor starts munching on the almonds as he's going over her tax returns. An hour later, he realizes that he's eaten all of them.

"I'm really sorry," he apologizes. "It's not bad enough I have to audit you, but then to eat all your almonds . . . I'm ashamed of myself."

"Oh, that's all right, sonny," the old lady says. "I already sucked all the chocolate off them."

So Harry is banging his best friend Sam's wife. Just as they're going at it hot and heavy, the phone rings.

The woman answers it, talks for a moment, then hangs up.

"That was Sam," she says.

"Shit!" Harry leaps out of the bed and starts grabbing his clothes.

"Don't worry," she says. "He just called to say he's out bowling with you."

Hear about the blind prostitute?

You really gotta hand it to her.

How do you know when a girl's really ugly?

She blindfolds herself before she takes a bath.

So the Polish judge says to the defendant, "You are charged with purse-snatching. How do you plead, guilty or not guilty?"

"Not guilty," the defendant replies.

"Then what the hell are you doing here? Go home," the Polish judge tells him.

Here about the rich Alabama businessman who died and put his estate in trust for his widow?

She can't touch it until she's thirteen.

How many mice does it take to screw in a lightbulb?

Two, if they're small enough.

Why does the Pope shower in a bathing suit?

He doesn't like to look down on the unemployed.

How can you spot Dolly Parton's baby?

It's the one with stretch marks on his lips.

What's the definition of a lap dog?

A really ugly girl who gives blow jobs.

"And what was the extent of the defendant's involvement in this matter?" the judge asked the woman bringing suit in the paternity case.

She replied, "Oh, I guess about six and a half inches."

Mary comes home from her third date with a dreamy guy and is on cloud nine. She gleefully rips off her clothes and tosses them all over the bedroom before flopping into bed and falling asleep.

The next morning, her mother says to her, "So, did you have fun last night?"

"It was all right," Mary replies.

"It must have been better than that," her mother says. "Your panties are still stuck to the ceiling."

The Puerto Rican girl is on the witness stand. The prosecutor says to her, "When you were being raped, did you scream for help?"

The girl nods.

The prosecutor asks, "And did anyone come?"

The Puerto Rican girl nods again. "First he did, then I did."

What did the rooster say to the hen?

"How do you want your egg this morning?"

Why is sex with husbands like a soap opera?

It's over just as things are getting interesting.

How can you tell when you have bad breath?

You walk into the dentist's office and he goes for the laughing gas.

How do you know when you're really a loser?

A whore says to you, "Sorry, not on the first date."

How do you know when a nuclear power plant isn't safe?

The billing department moves out.

Why do so many black girls miss the first day of school?

Morning sickness.

Two Polish teenagers really want to lose their cherries, so they go to the local whorehouse. Because it's Saturday and the place is really crowded, they have to take turns with one whore.

The hooker beckons the first Polack into the room and hands him a rubber.

"Put this on," she says. "So I don't get pregnant."

The first Polack puts on the rubber and has sex with the hooker. When he's done, the second Polack goes into the room. The hooker hands him a rubber and says, "Put this on so I don't get pregnant."

A week later, the first Polack says to his friend, "Do you really care if that whore gets pregnant?"

"Hell no," the friend says.

"Me neither," the first Polack says. "Let's take these rubbers off."

What's the difference between garbage and an ugly girl?

Garbage gets picked up at least once a week.

Hear about the slutty cheerleader?

She came home from the football game with a bad case of athlete's fetus.

So Murray and Irving are sitting on a park bench in Miami Beach. Irving says to Murray, "I'm seventy years old, I've got two million in the bank, and I'm in love with a blonde who's half my age. Do you think she'd marry me if I told her I was only fifty?"

Murray tells his friend, "I think you'd do a lot better if you told her you were eighty."

IN A WORD, SEX

Why is an impotent man like a Christmas tree?

The balls are both for show.

Why did Woody Allen go to see his physician?

He had diaper rash.

Why did the old lady piss all over her husband?

To celebrate their golden wedding anniversary.

For their fiftieth wedding anniversary, Harry and Gertrude returned to the hotel where they'd spent their honeymoon.

As they got ready for bed, Gertrude decided to put on the see-through two hundred dollar nightie she'd bought for the occasion. Only after she'd undressed did she realize that she'd left the nightie in the bathroom.

Stark naked, she tip-toed over to get it. Harry, who had taken off his glasses, looked at his wife and said, "For God's sake, Gertrude. For two hundred dollars they could've at least ironed it!"

Three secretaries discovered that they all had boyfriends with the same name—Stanley.

To avoid confusion, they decided to nickname the men after different sodas.

The first secretary said, "I'll name mine 7-Up, because he's got seven inches and it's always up."

The second secretary said, "I'll name mine Mountain Dew, because he loves my mountains and he sure can do it."

The third secretary said, "I'll name mine Wild Turkey."

"You can't do that," the first one says. "That's not a soda, it's a hard liquor."

"So is he," the third one replies.

Why are Peace Corps workers like plastic surgeons?

They both specialize in underdeveloped areas.

How many men does it take to screw in a lightbulb?

One—men will screw anything.

Why are tampons so popular all over the world?

They keep the Reds in, the Poles out, the Greeks happy, and the French hungry.

A trucker stops for lunch on I-95. He starts eyeballing the really good-looking waitress. She leans over to take his order, shoving her huge tits in his face.

"What would you like, sugar?" she says to him.

"I'd love a little pussy," he replies.

"So would I!" the waitress exclaims. "Mine's really huge."

Why don't most men care if women shave their pussies?

They don't mind going through the bush to get to the picnic.

What's green and smells like pork?

Kermit's finger.

What do you get when you cross an anteater and a vibrator?

An armadildo.

Heard about the new male birth control pill?

Take it the day after and it changes your blood type.

Morris, on his eightieth birthday, decides to fulfill a lifelong dream and go to a nudist colony.

No sooner does he sign in and shed his clothes than a gorgeous blonde comes over and gives him the best blow job of his life. Morris rushes back to the office and signs up for a year.

Walking around, he drops his cigar and bends over to pick it up. Before he can, a faggot dicks him up the butt.

Morris returns to the office and demands his money back.

"What happened?" the owner says. "I thought you were having a good time."

"Listen," Morris says. "I get excited once a month, but I drop my cigar five times a day!"

What's more boring than listening to a speech by Al Gore?

Watching Tipper undress.

Why did the necrophiliac cremate his girlfriend?

He wanted a piece of ash.

The sexaholic tells his psychiatrist, "I have a wife, a mistress, and four girlfriends. I love every type of sex there is, and I also love to jerk off and have wet dreams."

The shrink says to him, "Which type of sex do you love the best?"

He replies, "Masturbation. It feels good and you meet a much better class of people."

The young hooker reports for work on her first day at the whorehouse.

The madam says to her, "Do you have any questions?"

The hooker asks, "Yes. I was wondering how long dicks should be sucked."

The madam replies, "The same as the short ones, honey."

Hear about the Polish grandmother who went on the pill?

She didn't want any more grandchildren.

Then there's the flea who suffered from insomnia.

He only slept in snatches.

What do the president of Tupperware and a walrus have in common?

They both like a tight seal.

The deaf guy gets married and says to his new bride, "If you want sex and I'm asleep, just yank my dick twice."

"What if I don't feel like having sex?" his bride asks.

The deaf guy replies, "Then yank my cock fifty or sixty times."

Why is a cucumber better than a man?

Cucumbers stay hard for a whole week.

EVEN MORE GROSS ETHNIC JOKES

So the Polish girl walks into the local supermarket and says to the cashier, "Can you give me change for this fifty-dollar bill?"

The cashier replies, "This isn't a fifty-dollar bill, it's a soap coupon."

"My God, I've been raped!" the Polish girl cries.

Two Polish girls go to Fort Lauderdale for their vacation. The third day there, as they're lying in the sun, the first Polish girl says to her friend, "This suntan oil is useless."

"How do you know?" her friend asks.

"Because," the first Polish girl declares, "I've drunk three bottles of the stuff, and I'm still as pale as a sheet."

Why did the Italian girl go to see a dentist?

She wanted her wisdom teeth put in.

How can you spot a fashion-conscious Polish girl?

Her bowling shoes have high heels.

Why can't Italian girls give good head?

They can't get their lips over the guy's ears.

Hear about the Italian girl who was so fat, every time she had her picture taken she was charged group rates.

Two JAPs were walking down the street.

The first JAP said, "Would you believe it? I found a contraceptive on the patio yesterday."

The second JAP said, "What's a patio?"

How can you tell the Italian at the Off Track Betting parlor?

He's the one with the binoculars.

So the Polack walks into the bar and tells the bartender, "Give me five shots of whiskey."

The bartender pours out five shots of booze and says to the Polack, "What's the occasion?"

The Polack responds, "I'm celebrating my first blow job."

The bartender says, "Congratulations. The sixth drink is on the house."

"Forget it," the Polack declares, downing the first drink. "If five shots don't get the taste out of my mouth, six sure as hell won't."

How does a Polish Boy Scout start a fire?

By rubbing two matchsticks against each other.

How can you tell Italian toilet paper?

It has instructions printed on every sheet.

Why did the Polack spend three hours at the car wash?

He thought it was raining too hard to drive home.

What do Polacks call Cheerios?

Donut seeds.

What's the definition of an honest Polack?

A guy who works in a Turkish bath and never takes one.

So the Italian goes to see his unemployment counselor one January, and he is told, "The only work I can get you is driving a snowplow."

"What," the Polack says, "in this weather?"

A Polish woman is named as the other woman in an ugly divorce case. The prosecution lawyer says to her, "Do you admit that you went to a motel with this man?"

"Yes," the Polish woman replies, "but I couldn't help it."

"Why is that?" the lawyer asks.

"Because he deceived me." The Polish woman points to the husband.

"And how did he deceive you?" the lawyer asks.

The Polish woman replies, "He told the guy at the check-in desk that I was his wife."

When a Polish girl applies for a job as a bartender, the owner says to her, "Can you make a martini?"

"Yes," the Polish girl answers, "but if it's all the same to you, I don't like to fuck Italian guys."

What do black women and football players have in common?

They both shower after the fourth period.

Why do black women wear spiked heels?

To keep their knuckles from dragging on the sidewalk.

What does a public service announcement in Ebonics sound like?

"It's ten o'clock. Do *you* know what time it be?"

Why did the Polack cut a hole in his umbrella?

So he could tell when it stopped raining.

How can you tell a Polish pirate?

He's the one who has patches over both eyes.

What do you call a Polish brain surgeon?

A proctologist.

UTTERLY GROSS

What are the last ten things any man would ever say?

1. I think Barry Manilow is a cool motherfucker.
2. While I'm up, can I get you a beer?
3. I'm absolutely wrong. You must be right.
4. Her tits were just too big.
5. Sometimes I just need to be held.
6. That chick on *Murder She Wrote* gives me a hard-on.
7. No problem, I'd love to wear a rubber.
8. We haven't been to the mall in ages. Let's go, so I can hold your purse.
9. Screw football. Let's watch *Mad About You* instead.
10. We're lost. Let me stop and ask for directions.

So the distraught mother takes her six-year-old son to see a child psychiatrist. Seems the kid has been acting strangely. The shrink calls the woman into his office after examining the boy, and says, "Your son seems extremely disturbed by something you said to him, something about dying. What was it you said?"

The mother responds, "I told him that after we die, we get buried under a lot of dirt, then the worms come and eat our eyeballs and the ants eat your fingers and toes and everything else."

The shrink says, "That's terrible."

The mother says, "I guess, I should have told him the truth—that most of us go to hell and burn for eternity."

"Why didn't you?" the shrink asks.

"I didn't want to upset him," the mother says.

What's the worst part of democracy?

Any asshole can vote.

Why should you never throw a cigar butt in a urinal?

They get soggy and are hard to light.

How do you know when you're a cracker?

Your mother has more chest hair than your father.

What's another way of knowing you're a cracker?

Your sewer system consists of a pipe down a hillside.

How do you know when you're living in Alabama?

Your main source of income involves pigs or manure.

Late one night a burglar broke into a house he thought was empty. He tiptoed through the living room, then froze in his tracks when he heard a voice call out, "Jesus is watching you!"

All was silent again, so the burglar kept going. "Jesus is watching you!" the voice boomed again. The burglar stopped dead and started looking around. In a dark corner he spotted a bird cage. Inside was a parrot.

The burglar said to the parrot, "Was that you who said Jesus is watching me?"

"Yes," the parrot admitted.

"What's your name?" the burglar asked the bird.

"Murray," the parrot said.

"Murray!" the burglar exclaimed. "What moron named you that?"

"The same moron that named the pit bull Jesus," the parrot retorted.

Question: Are needles used for lethal injections sterilized first?

How do you pierce Oprah Winfrey's ears?

With a harpoon.

Why is buying a used car like going to a whorehouse?

Either way you're going to get screwed.

Why did the executive hire the prostitute to be his secretary?

On her application where it said "last position," the hooker wrote "doggie style."

How do you know when you have a really small dick?

Your girlfriend uses it as a toothpick.

What's the difference between a microwave and anal sex?

A microwave doesn't brown your cock.

What's the best way to remember dead relatives?

Put their ashes in your kid's Etch-A-Sketch.

What do you call men having sex with mannequins?

Guys in dolls.

A businessman in Chicago for a sales convention meets a beautiful blonde in a bar and persuades her to come up to his hotel room. She does, and he seduces her. Unfortunately, after they fall into bed, the businessman can't get it up.

His first night home, he steps out of the shower and walks into the bedroom. There lies his wife, her hair in curlers and wearing a ratty bathrobe, eating chocolates, and reading a soap opera magazine.

The businessman starts to get an erection. He looks down at his dick and says, "You ungrateful bastard. Now I know why they call you a prick."

Why is professional wrestling like watching Oral Roberts?

They're both fakes, but idiots watch them anyway.

What did the dumb nigger do when he won the lottery?

He bought a stretch limo and made a white guy sit in the back.

Two queers meet in a bar. The first one asks, "So how's your asshole, Jeremy?"

"Shut up, Stanley," Jeremy responds.

Stanley says, "Mine, too. Must be something going around."

The executive was flying first class on an airline that had just filed for bankruptcy. The flight attendant asked him, "Would you like dinner, sir?"

The exec inquired, "What are my choices?"

She responded, "Yes or no."

The old man was feeling a little run down, so he checked into the hospital for some tests. For three days and three nights, Epstein underwent every kind of test imaginable.

One night, a nurse came into his room and tried to get Epstein to have some soup. He was too tired to touch it, and fell asleep. His doctor decided that Epstein's problem was severe constipation. In the middle of the night, an orderly came into the room and gave Epstein a warm enema.

The next day, Epstein's wife came to visit him. "How are you feeling?" she asked.

"Pretty good," Epstein replied. "But if you ever have to come here, make sure you have the soup."

"Why?" his wife asked. "Does it make you healthy?"

"No," Epstein said. "But if you don't eat it, they make you take it up the ass."

Why did the eighty-year-old lady buy two candles?

In case she wanted to light one.

What was the hottest item in the convent?

The vibrating crucifix.

Hear about the family from Mississippi who went camping?

The mosquitoes threw up after biting them.

How can you tell when a woman is really flat chested?

She works in a topless bar as a busgirl.

The judge says to the burglar, "So you admit to breaking into the dress store four times?"

The burglar replies, "Yes, I do, your honor."

"Why did you break into the dress shop four times?" the judge demands to know.

"My wife wanted a dress," the burglar says.

"But you broke into the place four times!" the judge exclaims.

"I know," the burglar says. "My wife made me exchange it three times."

What's female, weighs three hundred pounds, and wears a lumberjack shirt?

Moby Dyke.

Two little brothers, ages six and eight, decide that it's time to learn how to swear. Billy says to Bobby, "You say 'shit' and I'll say 'fuck.' "

Excited, they rush down to breakfast, where their mother asks them what they want to eat.

Billy says, "Aw shit, I'll have the Cheerios."

Their mother beats the shit out of Billy and washes his mouth out with soap. She returns to the kitchen and asks Bobby what he wants for breakfast.

"I don't know," Bobby replies, "but it sure ain't gonna be those fuckin' Cheerios."

Why was the slutty chick nicknamed Baseball?

She was always getting thrown out at home.

What's the definition of a Republican?

Someone who loves the government for all it's worth.

What do you call ten blondes sitting in a circle?

A dope ring.

If Tarzan and Jane were Mexican, what would Cheetah be?

Pregnant.

How do you know when you're really poor?

The Salvation Army comes over and takes the wrong furniture.

How do you know when you're really, really poor?

You pull a string to turn on your lights.

Where do rich black people live?

In coon-dominiums.

Why are Mexicans like shooting pool?

You have to keep hitting them to get any English out of them.

How do you know when you're living below the poverty level?

You teach your children to play "Pull my finger."

Question: Do the Amish have phone books?

A husband and his wife love to play golf together, but neither of them is playing as well as they'd like to. They decide to take private lessons. The husband takes his lesson first. After seeing his swing, the pro says, "No, no. You're gripping the club too hard."

"Well, what should I do?" asks the husband.

The golf pro replies, "Hold the club gently, just like you'd hold your wife's tit."

The husband takes the pro's advice, takes a swing, and hits the ball 250 yards straight up the fairway.

The husband goes to his wife with the good news. The wife can't wait for her private lesson. The next morning, the pro watches her swing and says, "No, no, you're gripping the club way too hard."

"What should I do?" the wife asks.

The pro replies, "Hold the club gently, just like you'd hold your husband's cock."

The wife takes his advice and swings. The ball sputters maybe fifteen feet down the fairway.

The pro says, "Very good. Now take the club out of your mouth and swing it correctly!"

How can you tell when your girlfriend is having an orgasm?

Who gives a shit?

What do you call a girl who can suck a golf ball through a garden hose?

Darling.

SO GROSS EVEN WE WERE OFFENDED

Hear about the Newt Gingrich bucket meal at Kentucky Fried Chicken?

It's full of right wings and assholes.

So the lady calls the local police station and declares, "Officer, there's a Democrat masturbating in the window of the apartment across the alley!"

The cops asks her, "Lady, how do you know it's a Democrat?"

The lady says, "If it was a Republican, he'd be out screwing somebody!"

"So," the sportscaster asks the coach of the losing Miami Dolphins, "what do you think of your team's execution?"

The coach replies, "I'm all for it."

How do you know when you're really a slob?

There are more dishes in your sink than in your cabinet.

Joe and Ed are having beers at their local tavern.

Ed asks his friend, "So how was your blind date last night?"

Joe replies, "It was terrible. We had a nice dinner, then we drank some wine and sat down on the couch and started kissing. She seduced me and we made passionate love."

"What's so terrible about that?"

Joe says, "After we were done, she asked me to light her cigar."

What's the definition of a total loser?

A guy who loses his wife in a poker game.

What's another definition of a total loser?

Someone who wins first prize in a fart-off.

How do you know when your kid's a pervert?

He plays with the dog and dresses up like a fire hydrant.

What's the definition of Branson, Missouri?

Las Vegas for the toothless.

Why aren't niggers ever blonde?

They're dumb enough without it.

Why are blondes like computers?

You don't appreciate them until they go down.

What's the definition of a legal secretary?

A chick that's over eighteen.

Why do women fart after they piss?

They can't shake it, so they blow-dry it.

Why do farts smell?

So deaf people can enjoy them, too.

A man goes to a seedy hotel room with a prostitute. He's a little nervous, so he asks her, "Have you ever been picked up by the fuzz?"

"No," the whore says, "but if that's what you want, it'll cost you an extra fifty bucks."

The Polish woman calls the fire department and cries, "Hurry, our house is burning down!"

"Okay, lady," the fire chief says. "Just calm down and tell us how to get there."

The Polish woman responds, "Dammit, take that big red truck!"

What did the Polish mother tell her pregnant daughter?

"Don't worry. Maybe it's not yours."

The Polish kid was walking down the street and almost stepped in a pile of dog shit.

So delighted was he with his luck, he scooped up a handful of the dog shit and ran home. He burst into the house and said proudly to his father, "Look, Pa, what I almost stepped in!"

Why did the Polack stop moving his bowels?

He was afraid he'd forget where he put them.

What do you call a leper in a bathtub?

Stew.

So Epstein says to his physician, "Doctor, I've got five penises."

"My God! How do your pants fit?" the doctor asks him.

"Like a glove," Epstein says.

What do you give an elephant with diarrhea?

Lots of room.

Why do blind women masturbate with only one hand?

So they can moan with the other.

Moses comes back from Mount Sinai and says to the Jews, "I've got good news and bad news. The good news is, I got the Twelve Commandments knocked down to Ten Commandments. The bad news is, adultery is still in."

When Mrs. Hepplewhite goes to see her gynecologist, he helps her onto the table, then asks, "So what seems to be the problem?"

Mrs. Hepplewhite says, "Ever since you fitted me with that diaphragm, I've been pissing purple."

"My God!" the doc exclaims. "What kind of jelly are you using?"

"Welch's Grape," she tells him.

What's a transvestite's idea of a good time?

To eat, drink, and be Mary.